# Burlap Boutique

# Burlap *Boutique*

### charming accent wreaths
### & home décor

## KATIE CARTER

Fons&Porter

CINCINNATI, OHIO

# contents

# introduction

When I was approached to write this book, one of the first questions my publisher asked was, "Why burlap?" Why did so many of my designs incorporate this unique fabric? The more I thought about why I feel so strongly about this material, the more I realized just how simple, yet nuanced, my reasons are.

Burlap is a natural fabric with its roots in gardening and industrial manufacturing. It's rough, strong and durable. Moms like me need our decorations to last as long as possible and to stand up to not only the weather but also the occasional child treating it like a football and launching it across the room. With a material like burlap, you don't have to sacrifice pretty for practical.

Despite its rugged nature, burlap is incredibly easy to work with, making it perfect for beginners. Burlap is very forgiving, and the imperfections that often appear when tackling a new project are easily blended into the overall design. I strongly believe that true beauty doesn't hide its flaws—it embraces them.

Perhaps best of all, burlap is relatively inexpensive and available. You can find it at many craft stores and all over the Internet.

In short, I believe this wonder fabric is the perfect conduit to convey my love of design to the beginning DIYer.

# burlap basics

## TOOLS AND MATERIALS

Below are the tools and materials you'll want on hand to create the projects in this book.

**BURLAP** Like cotton fabric, burlap is a plant-based woven fabric. Made from jute or sisal plants, burlap is coarser than cotton but is durable and provides wonderful texture to projects made from it. The weave of the burlap affects its look and feel. Burlap with a looser weave, found at many craft and hobby stores, is coarser and more difficult to work with. Burlap with a denser weave, found at fabric stores and online shops, is smoother and easier to sew. For the projects in this book, I use Sultana burlap, a premium burlap that comes in a variety of colors and printed designs.

**FABRIC SCISSORS OR ROTARY CUTTER** I recommend using cheaper fabric scissors to cut burlap as the blades will dull quickly. You may also use a rotary cutter and cutting mat. I like using a rotary cutter when cutting out the small squares for the Burlap Bubble Wreath, page 56. The rotary cutter gets the job done quickly, and I am not worried about ruining my expensive fabric scissors.

**SEWING MACHINE AND NEEDLES** Sewing burlap is easy to do and allows you to create some great projects. Any sewing machine will work, but I recommend using an 18-gauge needle. Burlap can dull your needles quickly so have a few on hand. After sewing with burlap, thoroughly clean your machine, especially in the bobbin area. Little threads tend to go everywhere and may cause complications with your machine if not removed regularly.

**THREAD** Your average fabric thread will do just fine when sewing burlap.

Burlap is available in a wide variety of colors and prints.

Burlap layers can slip as you're sewing them, so use pins to keep them in place.

Keep your glue gun handy to attach bows and to make your projects more secure.

Use a permanent marker to trace shapes on burlap projects you don't plan to wash.

**STRAIGHT PINS** Burlap can be slippery, so use straight pins to keep the layers together as you sew or turn your machine speed to low.

**HOT GLUE GUN AND GLUE STICKS** In many of the projects in this book, the burlap is glued to itself or to a base. I prefer to use a hot glue gun with variable heat and glue sticks when working with burlap. Set the glue gun to low when gluing loosely woven burlap; if the glue seeps through, it won't be hot enough to burn your fingers. Set the glue gun higher when gluing several layers of burlap and when you need to use more than just a dot or two, as in the Garden Flag project on page 66.

**MARKER** When tracing on burlap, it's best to use a dark marker so you can clearly see the tracing lines. My personal favorite is a Sharpie; it's permanent so the ink won't run if the project gets wet. If you know you'll be washing your burlap project, however, you can use a washable marker.

**STENCILS** Densely woven burlap is a wonderful surface for stenciled designs. You can use stencils found at any craft store for the projects in this book. For more unique stencils, look for small sellers like those found on Etsy.

**SPRAY ADHESIVE** For an image with nice crisp edges, the stencil needs to be tacked firmly to the fabric. To do this, I spray Loctite adhesive spray to the back of the stencil (learn more about this technique on page 11).

**PAINT** Any acrylic paint you purchase at the craft store will work for stenciling. If you plan to wash your project, however, use paint specifically formulated for use on fabric instead.

**FOAM BRUSHES** Round foam brushes work well for stenciling; I use 1" (2.5cm) and 2" (5cm) sizes. For multiple projects or large projects, I use Plaid brand Spouncer Painters. These applicators are like a foam brush, but they attach directly to the bottle of craft paint, so there's no wasted paint. After you're done stenciling, remove the applicator, wash it off and use it again next time.

**TAPE MEASURE** Any tape measure for use with fabric will come in handy when working with burlap.

**FABRIC PROTECTOR** If your burlap project will be outside, you can protect the color from fading by spraying it with Ray Bloc by Trek7. This spray protects the project from UV damage and extends the life of the burlap.

# TECHNIQUES

Working with burlap is a bit different from working with cotton fabric because of burlap's coarse texture and loose weave. Here are some techniques that will help you achieve the best outcome for your burlap project.

### CUTTING BURLAP
Burlap is a woven fabric, so it naturally has vertical and horizontal thread lines. To prevent extra shedding and fraying, cut on the thread lines whenever possible.

### WASHING BURLAP
Because most of my projects won't be washed, I don't normally prewash my burlap. However, there are times when a project will be washed or maybe you just want a different look and feel to the fabric. In this case, wash the burlap to preshrink it before cutting. Wash on a gentle cycle and hang to dry. Know that your fabric will be wrinkled and look a bit of a mess at first. Don't worry though; a little steam from your iron or your garment steamer will remove the wrinkles.

  After preparing your burlap, I recommend using a damp cloth to wipe out your washing machine and wipe off your iron. The debris left behind by the burlap may alter or even ruin the next project you wash or iron.

### SEWING BURLAP
Because of the loose weave, burlap layers sewn together might start to come apart. Whenever a project or any area of a project will be exposed to wear or pulling, I use a zigzag stitch. When I make pillows, I use the zigzag stitch on either side of the opening I leave for turning the pillow right- +side out. For table runners and tree skirts that will be used regularly or that I want to last, I zigzag each raw edge.

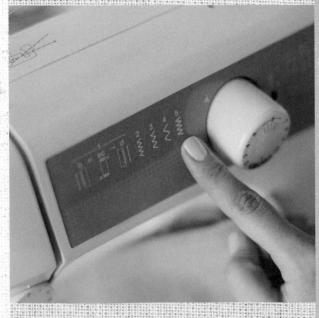

# Stenciling

To achieve clean edges on a stenciled image, use a spray adhesive to hold the stencil firmly to the burlap, and make sure there are no gaps between the stencil window and the fabric. Spray the stencil outdoors or in a well-ventilated area. After spraying the adhesive, allow the glue to dry until it is tacky. This takes approximately two minutes, depending on the temperature of your environment.

Don't start using the stencil while the glue is still wet. Doing so will make the stencil difficult to remove and could leave bits of glue on your burlap.

One spray of temporary adhesive should last for three or four impressions. When the tackiness starts to diminish, spray the stencil with a bit more adhesive.

To stencil, dab your paintbrush into the paint, then pounce the brush in an up-and-down motion over the stencil window. Be careful not to overload your brush with paint, as doing so may cause the paint to seep under the stencil. Continue to pounce the paint over the surface until you're satisfied with the coverage.

Remove the stencil while the paint is wet. If you leave the stencil on the burlap, the paint might seep underneath the stencil.

# Tying a Burlap Bow

I believe that everyone needs to know how to make a perfect burlap bow. There are just so many things you can use it for! The more creative you are with your bow, the more your projects will stand out.

**TO MAKE THIS BOW, YOU WILL NEED THE FOLLOWING:**

1½ yards (1.4m) of burlap ribbon 6" (15cm) wide

floral wire

scissors

tape measure

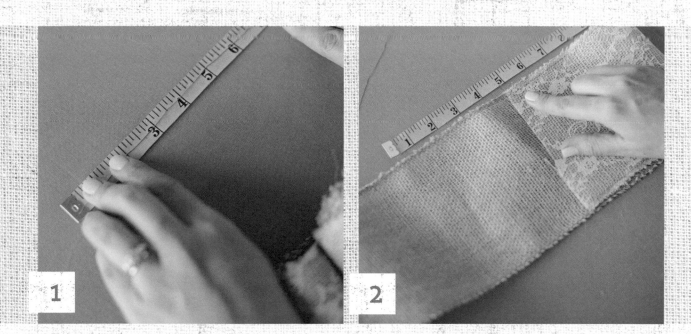

**1**

Measure and cut 8" (20cm) of floral wire.

**2**

Measure and cut 20" (51cm) of ribbon. Fold 5" (13cm) of one end of ribbon to the back of the ribbon. Repeat at the other end.

**3**

Overlap the second end over the first by ½" (1cm) and cut off the excess ribbon.

**4**

Pick up the ribbon at the center of its length and start pinching the ribbon together.

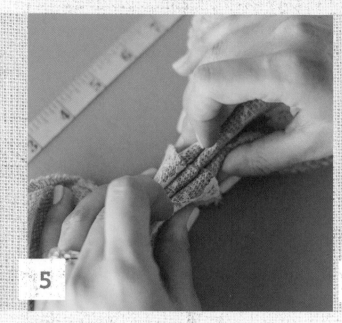

**5**

Continue pinching, making accordian-type folds, until you've gathered the width of the ribbon.

**6**

Hold the gathers firmly and wrap the wire around the center of the bow. Pull the wire tight and knot the ends to secure.

**7**

This is how the bow and wire should look at this point.

**8**

Cut another piece of the same ribbon to 20" (51cm).

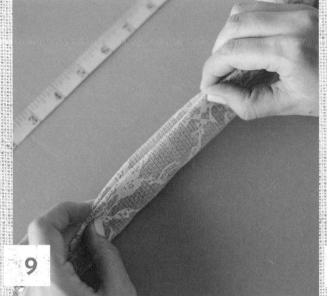

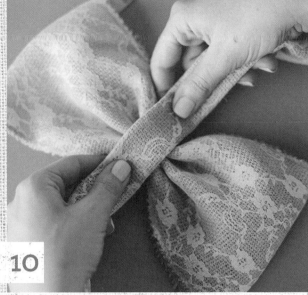

**9**

With the ribbon face down on your surface, find the center of the ribbon length. At the center, fold the long bottom edge up 1" (2.5cm) and the long top edge down 1" (2.5cm). Then fold the ribbon in half, meeting the two folded edges.

**10**

Center the folded ribbon over the wire at the front of the bow.

**11**

Tie the folded ribbon in a knot at the back of the bow. If your ribbon has a right side, turn the ribbon ends to the front. Trim the ends of the ribbon to the desired length. As you cut, follow the threads in the burlap to ensure the cut is straight.

Once you start making bows, you may not be able to stop! Add them to any project, including the Holiday Hoop Art project on page 90.

# at home

When creating personal space in your home, you want to put your own stylistic spin on it. The projects in this chapter will allow you to do just that. Place the lace-covered candles on your *Burlap-Covered Tray* or even inside a fireplace you aren't using. Add rustic beauty to your dining area with the *Ruffled Table Runner*.

# Lace
## CANDLE WRAPS

## MATERIALS LIST

candles in a variety of sizes

2–3 yards (1.8m–2.7m) assorted natural burlap ribbon, chevron burlap ribbon, lace burlap ribbon and lace ribbon

1 yard (0.9m) jute twine

hot glue gun and glue sticks

scissors

tape measure

Candles are a favorite for decorating no matter what your style. This technique of wrapping candles in burlap and lace instantly dresses up even the simplest candles.

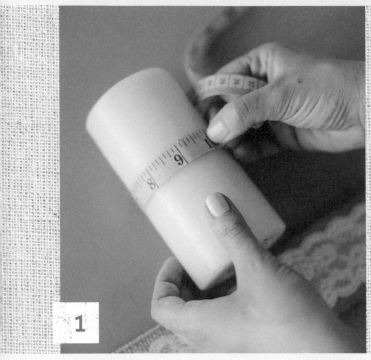

Measure the circumference of your candle.

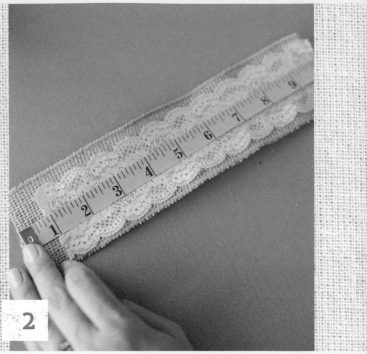

Cut a piece of natural burlap ribbon and a piece of lace to that length plus ½" (1cm).

Here the width of my burlap is 4" (10cm) and the width of my lace is 3" (8cm).

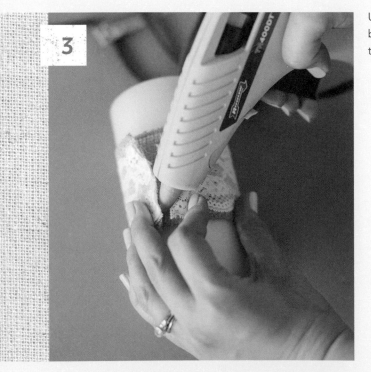

Use hot glue to glue both ends of the lace to the burlap ribbon. Wrap the ribbon around the candle and glue the ends to secure.

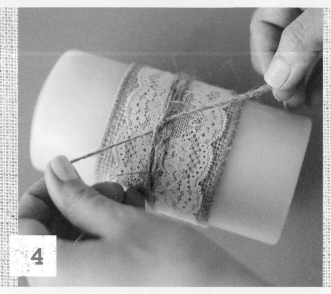

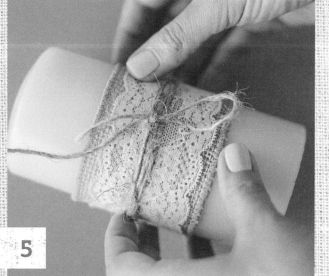

Cut a piece of twine to a length three times the circumference of the candle. Wrap the twine around the lace and knot the ends.

Tie the ends into a bow and make sure the burlap is centered on the candle.

Add interest and depth to your candle arrangement by using candles of different sizes. Here I used two 3" x 6" (8cm x 15cm) candles, two 3" x 9" (8cm x 23cm) candles and one 6" x 12" (15cm x 30cm) candle. Add variety with the wraps, too. Knot lace ribbon in the front of some and use chevron ribbon around others.

# Burlap-covered
## TRAY

**MATERIALS LIST**

16" × 22" (41cm × 56cm) tray

1 yard (0.9m) natural burlap

1½ yards (1.4m) white and natural striped ribbon

50–100 count upholstery nails

hot glue gun and glue sticks

adhesive spray

hammer

scissors

tape measure

Have you ever had a get-together and wanted a new or creative way to serve drinks or appetizers? Adding burlap to a wooden tray will transform any old or stained tray into a conversation piece.

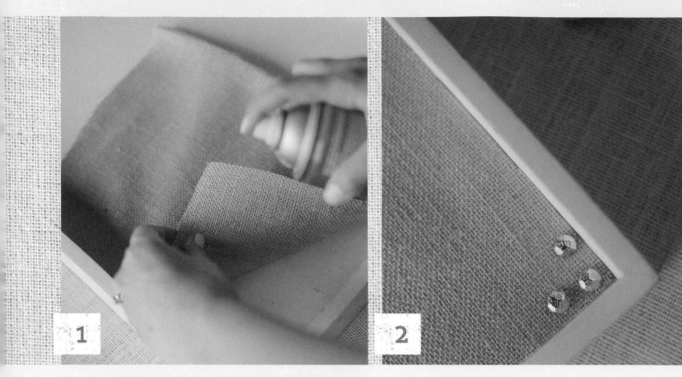

**1** Cut the burlap to fit the bottom of the tray. I cut my piece to 14" × 20" (36cm × 51cm).

Spray the back of the burlap with adhesive spray. While the glue is wet, place the burlap adhesive side down on the bottom of the tray. Press firmly and smooth out any wrinkles.

**2** Hammer upholstery nails around the perimeter of the fabric to secure the burlap piece. Space the nails about ½" (1cm) apart.

**3** Cut the striped ribbon to the same width as the inside side edges of the tray. Use hot glue to glue the ribbon to all four inside edges of the tray.

# Stenciled
## PLACE MAT

### MATERIALS LIST

1 yard (0.9m) natural burlap

tan thread for sewing machine

navy and white craft paint

removable adhesive for stencil

round foam brush

letter stencil

circle stencil

scissors

tape measure

sewing machine

This burlap place mat is a quick way to change the look of your dining room or kitchen table. Update your place mats seasonally using different colors and images.

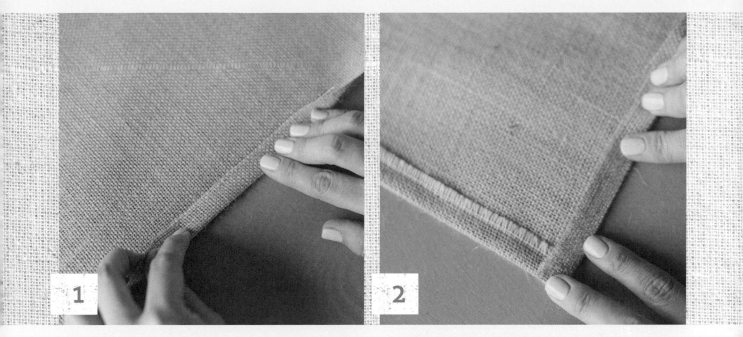

1

Cut a piece of burlap to 15" × 21" (38cm × 53cm) for each place mat you'll be making. Fold the short ends over ½" (1cm) to the back of the burlap and pin them.

2

Sew the folded edges using a straight stitch on your sewing machine. Fold the long edges of each place mat over ½" (1cm) to the back of the burlap and pin them.

3

Use the same stitch to sew down these folded edges

4

Find the center of the place mat and temporarily adhere the letter stencil to that spot. Dip the foam brush in navy paint and pounce the brush over the stencil to paint the letter. Let the paint dry, then repeat with the circle stencil and white paint. For more on stenciling, see page 11.

# Ruffled
## TABLE RUNNER

**MATERIALS LIST**

2 yards (1.8m) white burlap

white thread for sewing machine

tape measure

scissors

straight pins

sewing machine

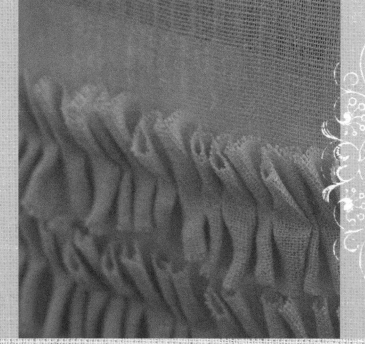

Who doesn't love a few ruffles here and there?
Add a couple rows of ruffles to any runner, and
they automatically turn ho-hum into adorable.
The rows of burlap ruffles on this soft white
burlap runner make it pretty and sophisticated.

Cut a 15" × 73" (38cm × 185cm) piece of burlap for the table runner base.

Fold all four edges over ½" (1cm) and sew the folds with a straight stitch on your sewing machine.

For the ruffles, cut four strips 3" (8cm) wide.

Cut each strip 28" (71cm) long.

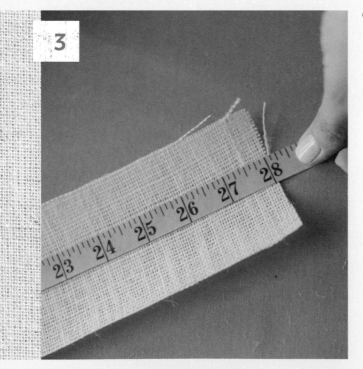

Pin one end of a strip to one end of the table runner with the strip parallel to the width of the runner. Pinch and bunch the strip across the width of the runner, pinning in place as you go. At the opposite side, align the opposite end of the strip to the edge of the runner.

Sew the strip to the runner with a straight stitch down the center of the strip.

Pin and sew a second strip directly above the first strip. Then repeat on the other short end of the runner.

# Burlap
## GARLAND

## MATERIALS LIST

20–30 strips assorted burlap ribbon and fabric at least 2" × 18" (5cm × 46cm)

1½ yards (1.4m) jute rope twine

scissors

tape measure

This spunky garland is just what you need to liven up any dull space in your home. I love making mini garlands to hang over empty picture frames or above a doorway.

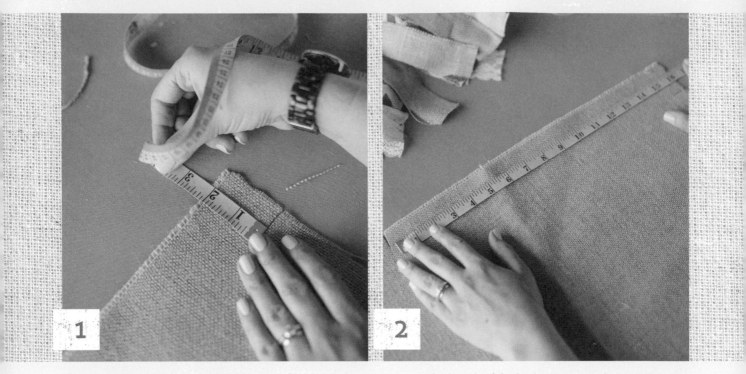

**1** Measure 2" (5cm) from the edge of a piece of burlap and make a small cut to mark the width.

**2** Measure the length of the burlap strip to either 16" (41cm) or 18" (46cm), depending on how long you want the ties to be. Make a small cut at that measurement, then cut out the burlap strip. Cut between twenty and thirty strips.

Wrap one strip around the twine.

**3**

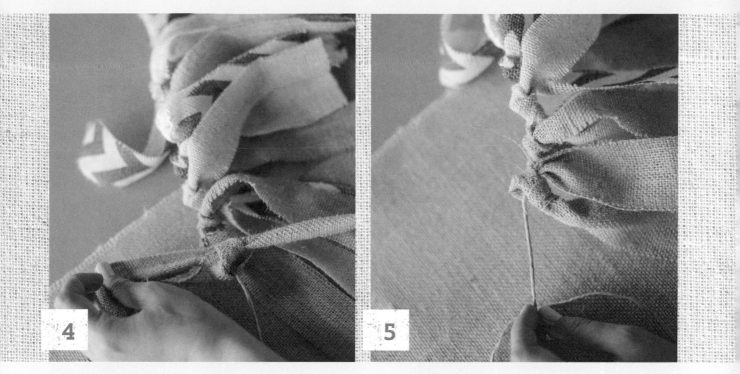

**4** Tie the ends of the strip in a knot to secure it.

**5** Repeat steps 3 and 4 for the length of the twine, leaving a few inches (centimeters) at each end uncovered so you can hang it easily.

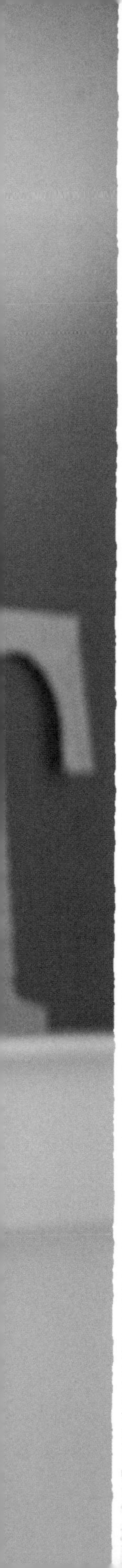

# Decorative
## LETTERS

## MATERIALS LIST

12" (30cm) chipboard or wooden letters

1 yard (0.9m) gray burlap

clear decoupage medium

foam brush

marker

scissors

There are days when my house simply feels like it needs a little change. By adding a letter here or there, you can quickly add interest to any space. Put four burlap letters together, however, and you have a focal point!

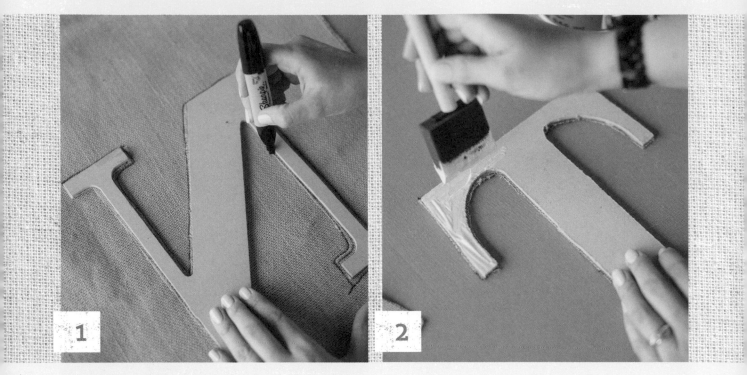

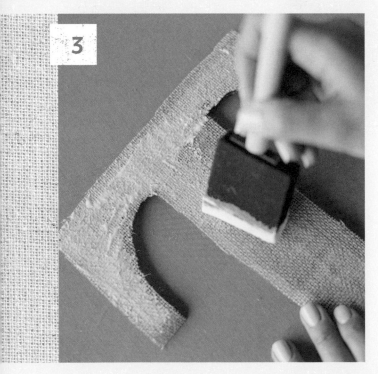

Place a chipboard letter face down on the burlap (it will be backward). Trace around the letter with a marker.

Cut out the letter from the burlap. Use a foam brush to apply decoupage medium over the front of the chipboard letter.

Place the burlap letter onto the medium and smooth it with your fingers to remove any bubbles or wrinkles. Brush another layer of decoupage medium over the burlap. Let it dry until the medium is clear, or let it dry overnight.

This holiday letter adds cheer to your outdoor décor. Glue printed Christmas burlap over a letter shape and hot glue a red chevron burlap ribbon to the back.

# Picture frame
## JEWELRY HOLDER

### MATERIALS LIST

old frame of any size (18" × 24" [46cm × 61cm] shown)

1 yard (0.9m) chicken wire

½ yard (0.5m) gray burlap

white spray paint

hot glue gun and glue sticks

hanging hardware

automatic stapler and staples

hammer

wire cutters

scissors

If you're like me, you're always searching for that missing earring in your jewelry box. This chicken wire frame is elegant and makes it easy to find exactly what you are looking for in no time.

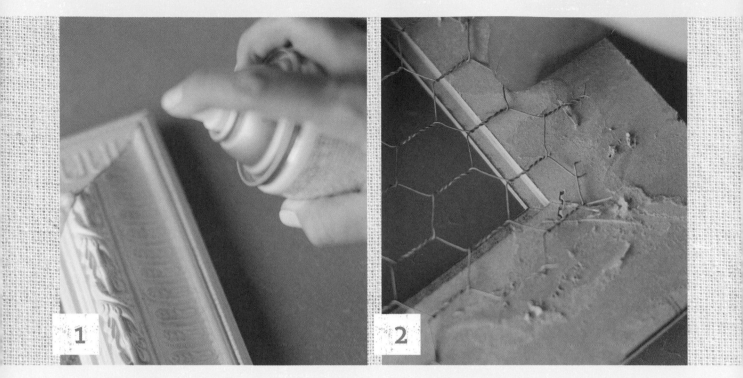

**1** Paint the frame with two coats of spray paint, allowing the paint to dry between coats.

**2** Measure the opening of the frame and add 2" (5cm) to the width and the length. Cut the chicken wire to this measurement. Use the automatic stapler to secure the chicken wire to the back of the frame.

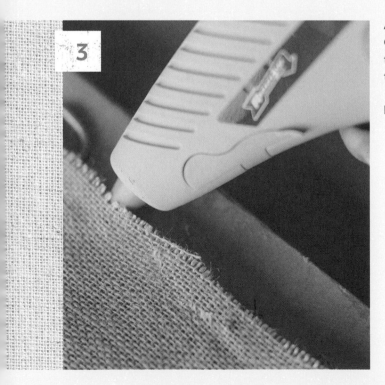

**3** Add 1" (2.5cm) to the length and width of the chicken wire. Cut the burlap to this size. Use hot glue to glue the burlap to the back of the frame, over the chicken wire. Pull the burlap taut for a smooth look.

Attach hanging hardware to the back of the frame with a hammer.

# wreaths

I think everyone needs at least one wreath in their home—I have them everywhere in mine! Try placing a wreath on a bookshelf by sitting it upright in one of the shelves or hang one on your back porch to liven it up a bit. I love changing out my wreaths to coordinate with the different seasons as well as the holidays! Here are some fun and whimsical ideas for getting crafty with wreaths.

# Fabric floral
## WREATH

### MATERIALS LIST

14" (35cm) straw wreath

variety of burlap pieces, each at least 3" × 24" (8cm × 61cm)

Approximately 7' (2.1m) natural burlap ribbon 4" (10cm) wide

1 yard (0.9m) lace burlap ribbon

floral pins

hot glue gun and glue sticks

tape measure or yardstick

If you love the art of wreath making, this wreath tutorial is for you. Wow your friends and family with this simple but beautiful burlap rose wreath.

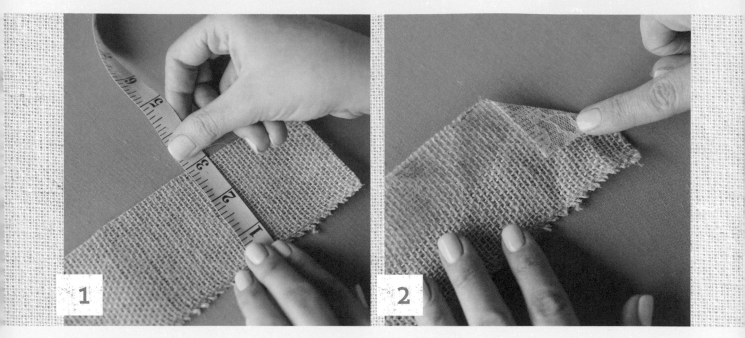

**1**

To make a rose, cut a burlap piece to 3" × 24" (8cm × 61cm).

**2**

With the burlap face down on your work surface, fold the top corner toward the center of the ribbon.

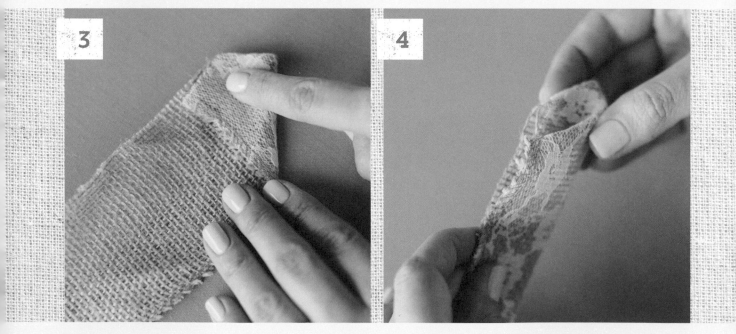

**3**

Fold the opposite top corner over the first fold, matching the corner to the left edge.

**4**

Fold the folded end of the strip in half lengthwise.

Burlap boutique

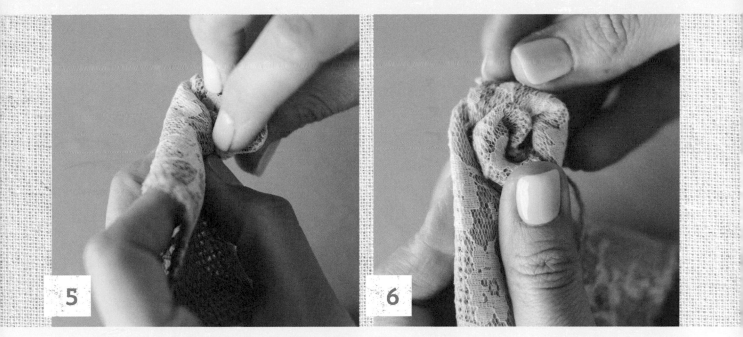

**5** Holding the folded end, twist the strip clockwise to form the center of the rose.

**6** Continue twisting the burlap strip clockwise and folding the strip in half lengthwise.

Continue until you reach the desired flower size. The roses in this project measure between 3" (8cm) and 3½" (9cm) wide.

**7**

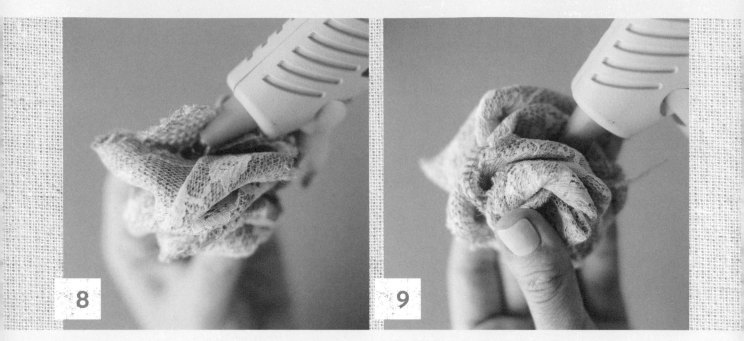

**8**

Place hot glue between the lower layers to secure them in place.

**9**

Glue the upper layers in place as well.

Repeat steps 1–9 until you reach the desired quantity of roses. For this wreath, I made a total of six roses using natural burlap ribbon and lace burlap ribbon.

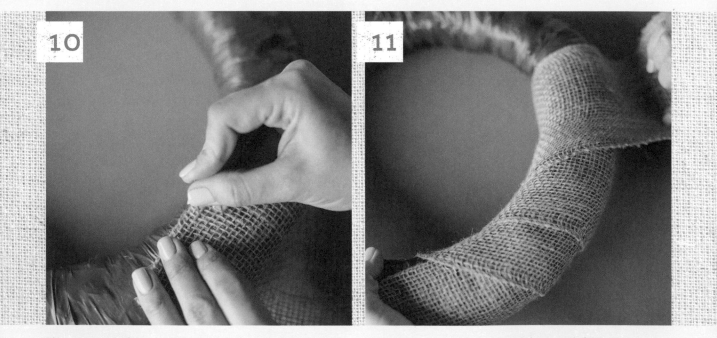

**10**

Place one end of the natural burlap ribbon on the wreath form and pin in place with a floral pin.

**11**

Wrap the natural ribbon around the wreath form. Overlap the edges so all of the form is covered. Once covered, trim the opposite end of the ribbon and pin to secure.

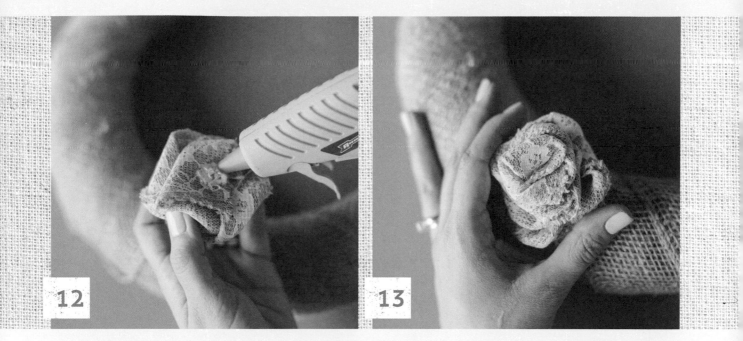

Place hot glue on the bottom of a rose.

Place the rose on the wreath. Repeat for all the roses. Note that I clustered my roses in the lower left side of the wreath.

Cut the lace ribbon to 36" (91cm). Thread one end of the ribbon through the wreath and tie the ends into a knot for hanging.

# Moss & cross
## WREATH

## MATERIALS LIST

14" (36cm) moss wreath form

8" × 11" (20cm × 28cm) natural wooden cross

2 yards (1.8m) natural nonwired burlap ribbon 4" (10cm) wide

floral wire

floral pins

dark furniture wax

cream craft paint

foam paintbrush

furniture wax brush

dry cloth

hot glue gun and glue sticks

scissors

tape measure

Spring is a wonderful season with warming temperatures and blooming flowers. But it quickly reminds you that the outside of your home needs a little sprucing. Hang this earthy moss wreath with faux-finished cross on your front door, and you'll be on your way to welcoming spring.

**1** Use a foam brush to paint a single layer of cream paint on the front and back of the wooden cross. Allow it to dry.

**2** Prepare to give the cross more dimension by dipping your wax brush into the dark wax.

Brush the wax onto the front of the cross. Make sure to brush the wax onto the raised areas of the cross. Then quickly rub the cross with a dry cloth to remove any excess wax.

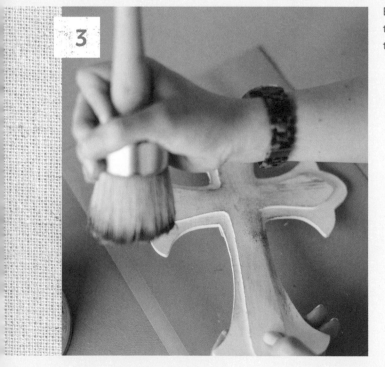

**3**

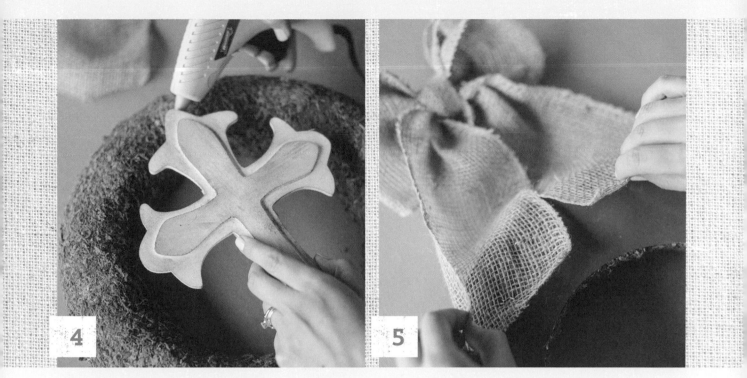

**4** Glue the cross to the front of the wreath; place glue at the top and bottom of the wreath so the cross is well secured.

**5** Make a bow with the burlap ribbon following the instructions on pages 12–15. Place the bow face down on your work surface and find the center top of the wreath.

Use floral pins to secure the bow ends to both sides of the center point of the top of the wreath. Use three or four floral pins on each side. Hang the wreath by the bow.

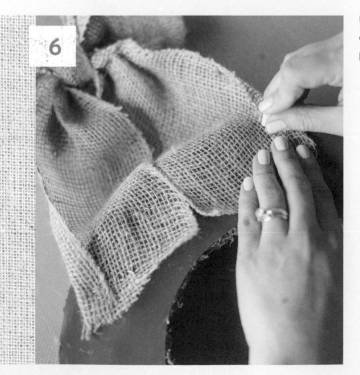

**6**

# Burlap bubble
## WREATH

## MATERIALS LIST

14" (36cm) straw wreath

3 yards (2.7m) burlap in any color

1½ yards (1.4m) chevron burlap ribbon

floral wire

floral pins (100 count)

scissors

tape measure

Everyone needs a burlap bubble wreath in their life! It's perfect for your front entry as a welcome wreath to greet guests entering your home.

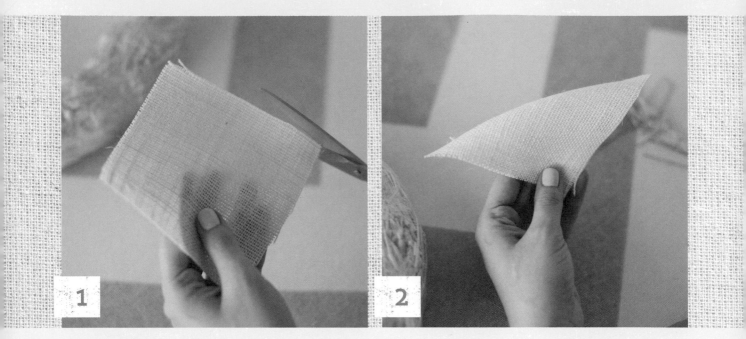

**1** Measure 2 yards (1.8m) of the burlap and cut all of it into 4" × 4" (10cm × 10cm) squares.

**2** Fold one burlap square corner to corner to create a triangle.

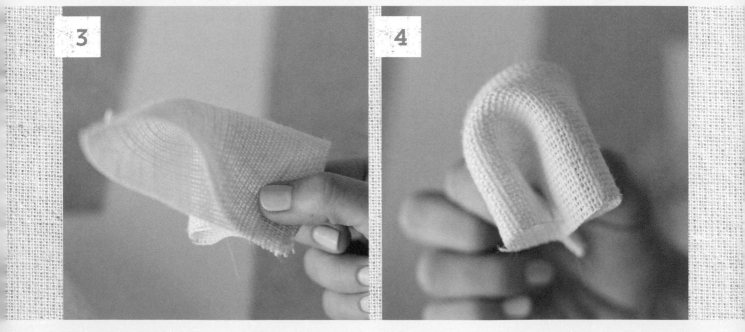

**3** While holding the first two corners, fold the right-hand corner of the triangle to the back and match it to the first two corners.

**4** Repeat with the left-hand corner, so all four corners are pinched between your fingers. This is the burlap bubble.

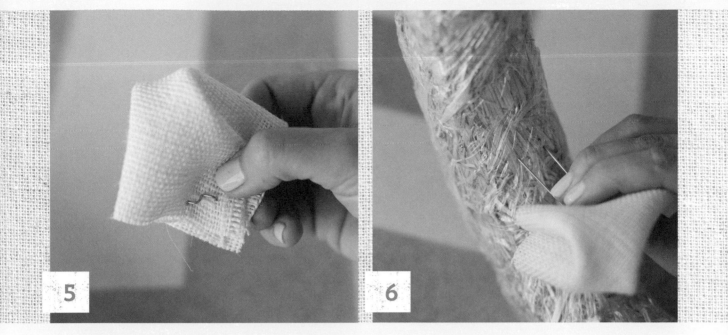

**5** Place a floral pin at the base of the bubble to hold its shape.

**6** Insert the pin and bubble into the inside edge of the straw wreath.

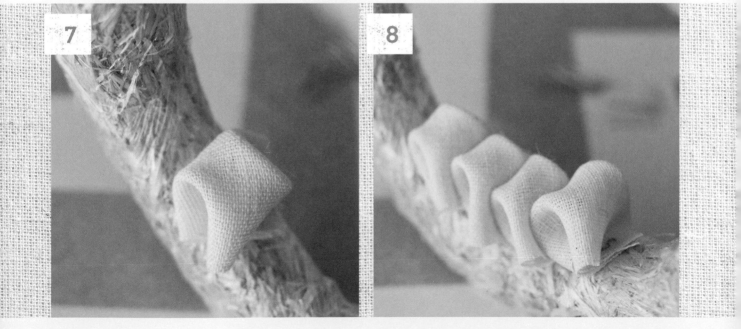

**7** You've completed your first burlap bubble!

**8** Continue to fold the squares and attach them to the inner edge of the wreath, placing each bubble about 1" (2.5cm) apart. Cover the entire inner edge of the wreath.

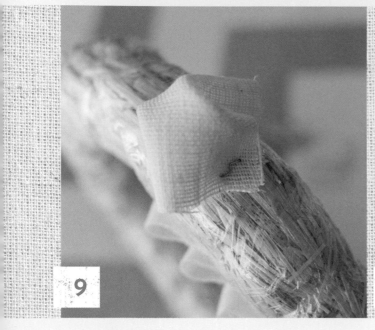

**9**

Fold another burlap square and attach it to the outer edge of the wreath.

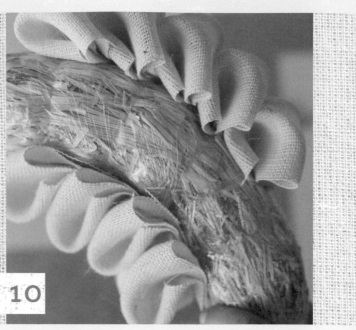

**10**

Continue to add folded squares until the outer edge is filled.

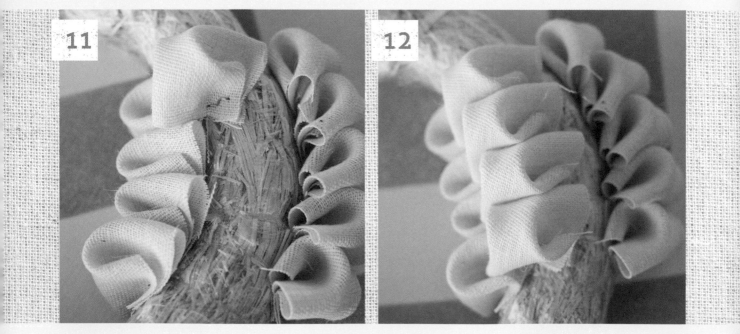

**11**

Place the wreath on your work surface with the front facing up. Begin a third row of squares on the wreath close to the inner edge. Note that three rows of squares will be added to the wreath front.

**12**

Continue to add squares to fill this row.

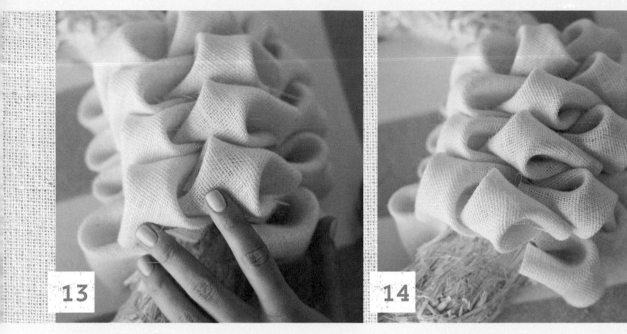

Add another row of squares next to the previous row.

Add your final row of squares between the previous row and the outer edge of the wreath. As you fill this row, fill in any gaps you might see.

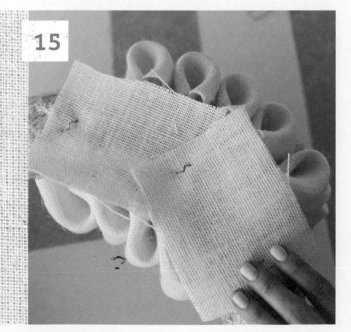

Use any remaining burlap squares or cut burlap of a similar size to cover the back of the wreath. Secure the burlap with floral pins.

Make a bow with the chevron burlap ribbon following the instructions on pages 12–15. Attach the ribbon to the wreath with floral pins.

*The Burlap Bubble Wreath* is extremely versatile.
Use red burlap for a Valentine's Day wreath. Add a
glitter-covered X and O with hot glue. A pink and
natural burlap ribbon bow finishes the look.

Use a mix of colored burlap to make this Fourth of July wreath. Place red and white burlap bubbles on the bottom two-thirds of the wreath. Wrap navy burlap ribbon around the top one-third and add German glass glitter stars with hot glue.

# gifts to give

If you're like me, you always need a gift for someone , be it a housewarming gift, birthday gift, congratulations gift or just a thank-you gift. Here are some of my favorites for every occasion.

# Garden
## FLAG

## MATERIALS LIST

½ yard (0.5m) natural burlap fabric

3 yards (2.7m) natural burlap ribbon 3" (8cm) wide (wired or nonwired)

1 yard (0.9m) burlap chevron ribbon

floral wire

black craft paint

tan thread for sewing machine

removable adhesive for stencil

hot glue gun and glue sticks

foam paintbrush

stencil

tape measure

sewing machine

scissors

straight pins

This garden flag makes a great house-warming gift. What is better than a cute handmade gift that is also personalized?

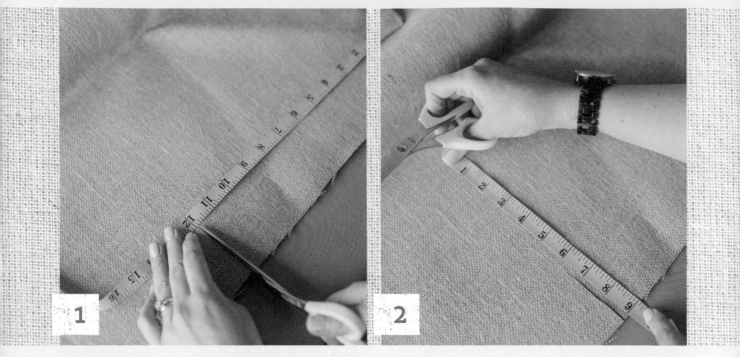

**1** Following the grain of the fabric, make a small cut at 12" (30cm).

**2** Again following the grain, measure 9" (23cm) from the long edge. Cut out this piece of burlap then cut out a second piece measuring 9" × 12" (23cm × 30cm).

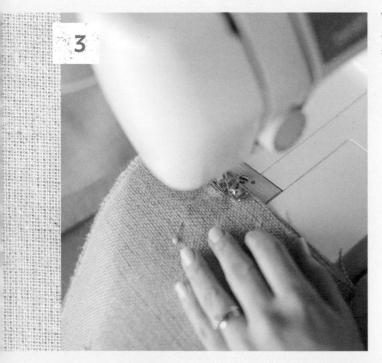

**3** With wrong sides facing, place one piece over the other and pin the edges. Sew around all four edges with a straight stitch and ¼" (6mm) seam allowance.

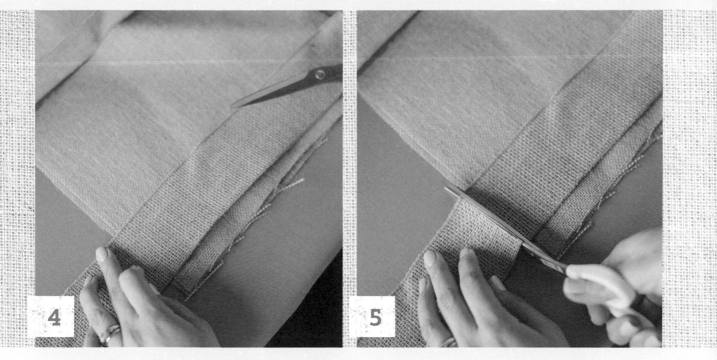

Cut two pieces of natural burlap ribbon to 8" (20cm). Cut two pieces of the ribbon to 12" (30cm), using the long edge of the sewn pieces as a guide.

Cut two pieces of the burlap ribbon to 9" (23cm), using the short edge of the sewn piece as a guide.

Fold the 12" (30cm) ribbon in half lengthwise. Wrap the ribbon around one long edge of the sewn piece.

Pin the ribbon in place. Repeat with the other 12" (30cm) ribbon on the other long edge.

Sew both ribbons in place with a straight stitch.

Fold the two 9" (23cm) pieces of ribbon in half and sew them to the top and bottom of the flag, as described in steps 6–8.

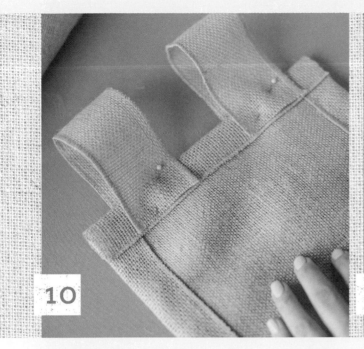

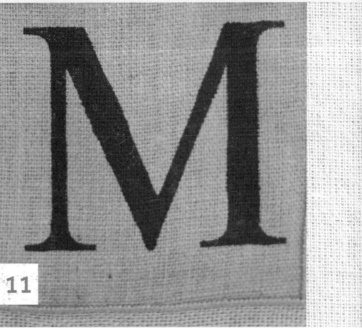

**10**

Fold one 8" (20cm) ribbon in half as shown. Place one short edge of the ribbon on the front of the flag and one on the back. Align the left edge of the ribbon with the ribbons attached to the flag. Pin the ribbon in place. Repeat with the second piece of ribbon on the right side of the flag.

Sew the short ends of the ribbon to the flag with one line of straight stitching at the base of the ribbon and a second line 1" (2.5cm) above that.

**11**

Place the letter stencil on the front of the flag slightly below center from top to bottom. Secure the stencil with temporary adhesive spray. Dip the foam brush into the black paint and pounce the paint over the stencil to fill in the letter shape. Let the paint dry. For more on stenciling, see page 11.

**12**

Make a bow following the steps on pages 12–15 with the chevron ribbon. Attach the bow to the top center of the flag with hot glue.

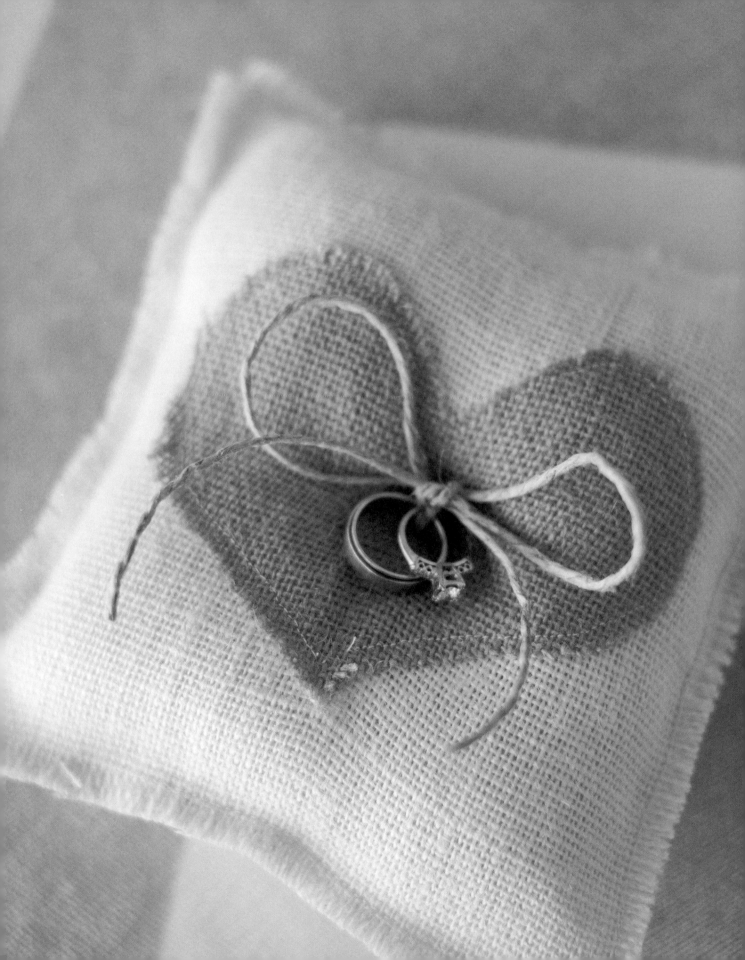

# Ring
## PILLOW

## MATERIALS LIST

¼ yard (23cm) white burlap

7" (18cm) square gray burlap

14" (36cm) jute rope twine

fiberfill

white and gray thread for sewing machine

marker

scissors

tape measure

straight pins

sewing machine

This sweet and simple ring pillow is ideal for any bride. Coordinate the color of the burlap with the wedding colors for a flawless look.

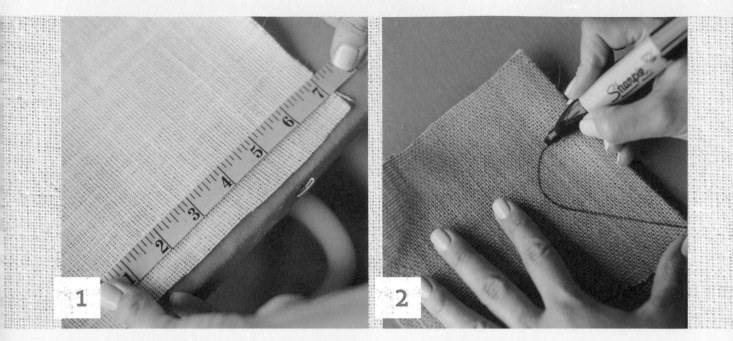

**1**

Cut two pieces of white burlap to 7" × 7" (18cm × 18cm).

**2**

Cut a piece of gray burlap to the same size as the white squares. Fold it in half. Draw half a heart on the fold line with a marker.

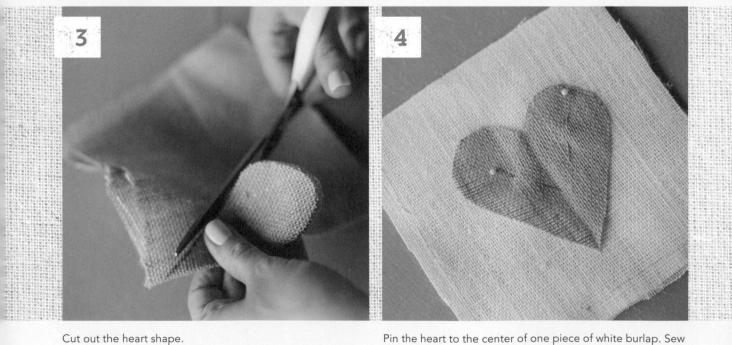

**3**

Cut out the heart shape.

**4**

Pin the heart to the center of one piece of white burlap. Sew around the heart with gray thread and a straight stitch. Use a ¼" (6mm) seam allowance.

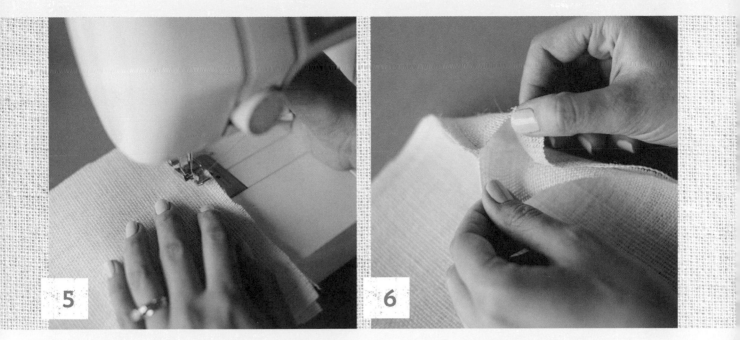

**5** With wrong sides facing, pin the two squares together. Sew around the perimeter of the squares with a straight stitch and ½" (1cm) seam allowance. Stop stitching 2" (5cm) from where you started.

**6** Use the space you left open to add the fiberfill.

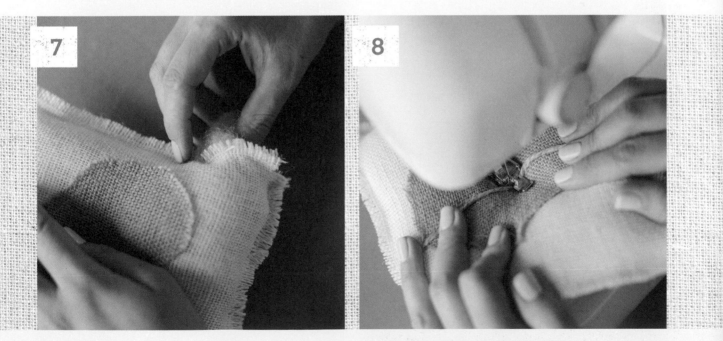

**7** Fill the pillow with fiberfill. Sew the opening of the pillow closed with your sewing machine.

**8** Fold the twine in half and place it on the center of the heart. Sew the twine to the pillow with a zigzag stitch on your sewing machine, if you're able. If not, sew the twine to the heart by hand.

# Special date

## PILLOW

### MATERIALS LIST

1½ yards (1.4m) white burlap fabric

white sewing machine thread

gray and red craft paint

number stencils

small heart stencil

round foam brush

temporary adhesive

scissors

tape measure

sewing machine

straight pins

14" × 20" (35.6cm × 50.8cm) pillow form

If you're like me, shopping for a couple's wedding gift can be challenging. Why not give them something special to remind them of their wedding day?

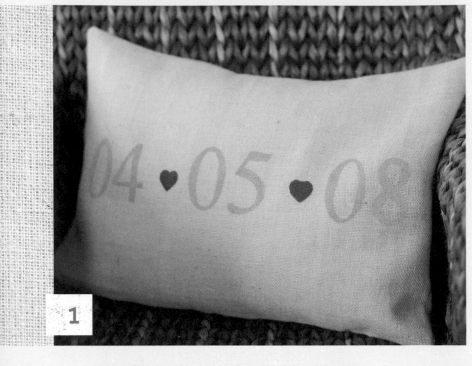

Cut one piece of burlap to 16" × 22" (41cm × 56cm). Cut two pieces of burlap to 13" × 16" (33cm × 41cm).

Stencil the date onto the larger piece of burlap, centering it as desired. With the foam brush, use gray paint for the date and red paint for the hearts. For more on stenciling, see page 11.

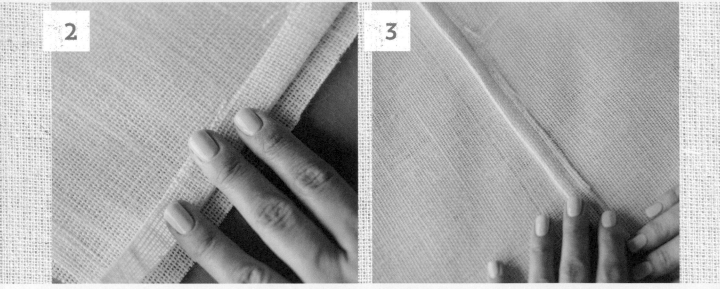

Fold one 16" (40.6cm) edge of one smaller piece of burlap over ½" (1cm) and pin. Repeat for one side of the second piece of burlap. Sew the folds down with a straight stitch using your sewing machine.

Place the stenciled burlap face up on your work surface. Align the unsewn 16" (40.6cm) edge of one piece of burlap to the right edge of the center; place the smaller piece face down. Repeat with the second smaller piece of burlap on the left side of the center piece. The two smaller pieces will overlap each other on top of the stenciled piece. Make sure the top and bottom edges are aligned as well.

Use a zigzag stitch to sew all around the perimeter of the pillow layers. Turn the pillow right side out through the slit between the two smaller pieces of burlap. Insert the pillow form through the slit.

# State
## ART

## MATERIALS LIST

14" × 14" (36cm × 36cm) wooden frame

1 yard (0.9m) burlap fabric

8 silver upholstery nails

white, gray and red craft paint

temporary adhesive

state stencil

small heart stencil

letter stencils

hanging hardware

round foam brush

scissors

tape measure

rubber mallet

automatic stapler and staples

It's always good to be reminded of where you came from. This piece of artwork makes a wonderful going-away gift for a college student, a neighbor or a co-worker. It's a fun way to remind them that the people at home care.

**1** Lay your wooden frame directly onto the burlap. Mark the outline of the frame, then add 2" (5cm) to each side. Cut out the burlap.

Place the state stencil on the burlap as desired and stencil with the gray paint and foam brush. Let the paint dry for about ten minutes between layers. Stencil the heart with red paint; stencil the letters with white paint. Let the paint dry overnight or at least eight to twelve hours.

**2** Place the burlap over the frame and make sure the stencil is centered. Pull the edges of the burlap to the back of the frame and staple it onto the frame. Pull the burlap as taut as you can.

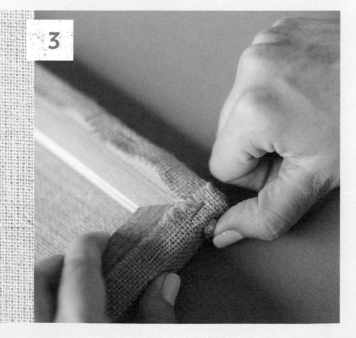

**3**

Use the rubber mallet to place upholstery nails on both sides of each corner of the frame, then attach the hanging hardware.

# holidays

Fun and personal décor never fails to add a sense of comfort to the holidays. Creating the pieces yourself brings an even warmer feeling to your family get-togethers. These seasonal home décor projects will surely do just that!

# Give Thanks
## BANNER

## MATERIALS LIST

1 yard (0.9m) burlap fabric

3 yards (2.7m) jute rope twine

brown and cream craft paint

foam round brush

temporary spray adhesive

alphabet stencils

hot glue gun and glue sticks

triangle pattern on page 106

Pennants and banners are commonly used to express team loyalty or celebration. Here you'll use the banner form to communicate a heartfelt expression. Using the special technique demonstrated in this project, your letters will stand out more than they would on natural burlap.

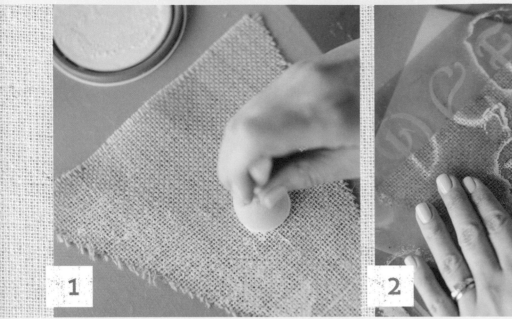

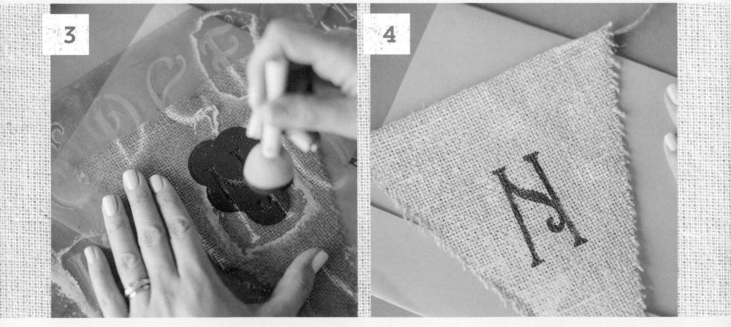

**1** Using the pattern on page 106, cut out one triangle for each letter of your message from the burlap (I cut out ten triangles). Place a small amount of white paint on the sponge brush and slowly pounce paint in the center of each triangle, leaving the edges unpainted. Let dry.

**2** Spray temporary adhesive on the back of the stencil. Select the first letter of your message from the letter stencil and center the letter over one triangle. Make sure the horizontal edge of the triangle is at the top.

**3** Place a small amount of brown paint onto the foam brush. Holding the stencil firmly with one hand, pounce the brush in an up-and-down motion onto the stencil to fill in the letter.

**4** Remove the stencil and allow the paint to dry. Continue stenciling one letter onto each triangle to spell out your message.

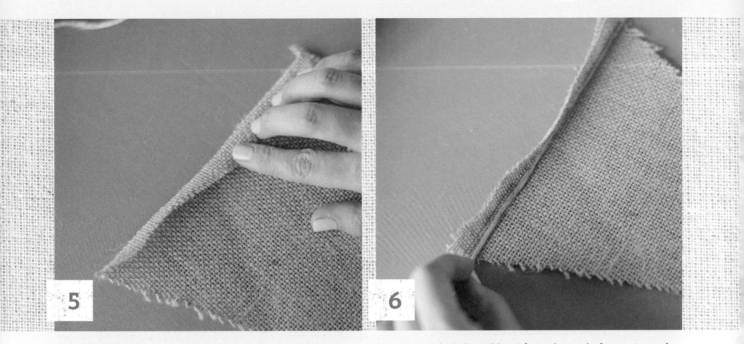

**5**

Cut one piece of twine to 35" (89cm) and a second piece to 45" (114cm). Fold the top edge of your first triangle over ½" (1cm) to the back and press the fold with your fingers.

**6**

Measure 6"–9" (15cm–23cm) from the end of one piece of twine (to provide enough space at the end for hanging). Place the twine inside the fold of the triangle, leaving the end of the twine loose for hanging (the length of twine you use will depend on the length of your word).

**7**

Run hot glue along the fold of the triangle and fold the edge over the twine. Glue the next triangle about 2" (5cm) from the first. Continue adding triangles. Place four triangles on the shorter piece of twine and six on the longer piece of twine.

This banner is wonderfully versatile. Cut circles of
chalkboard fabric and sew them onto burlap triangles with a zigzag stitch. Use chalk to write a new
message every season. Here I've tied lace between
the triangles for a festive look.

Mini banners look great as a topper for a wedding cake or bridal shower dessert. Reduce the size of the triangles, glue the top edge directly to the twine and attach the twine ends to bamboo skewers. Easy and adorable!

# Holiday
## HOOP ART

## MATERIALS LIST

14" (36cm) embroidery hoop

½ yard (.5m) printed burlap

1½ yards (1.4m) red chevron burlap ribbon

white craft paint

floral wire

temporary spray adhesive

round foam brush

alphabet stencil

hot glue gun and glue sticks

tape measure

marker

scissors

It's fun to use ordinary objects to make something spectacular. With printed burlap and an
embroidery hoop, you can create a welcoming
wreath to greet guests entering your home. Try
gathering an odd number of hoops in different
sizes to hang on a wall for a dramatic look.

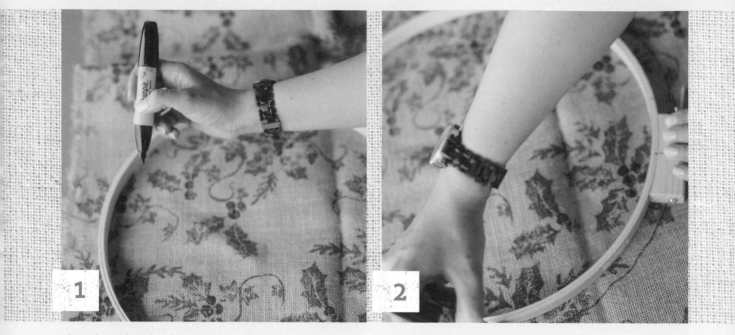

**1**

Place the embroidery hoop onto the front of the burlap.

**2**

With your marker, trace ½" (1cm) from the outside edge of the hoop.

**3**

Cut out the circle on the marked line. If desired, stencil a message on the burlap, following the instructions on page 11. Allow the paint to dry.

Unscrew the hoop and remove the inner hoop. Center the burlap circle over the inner hoop.

**4**

Place the outer hoop over the inner hoop and pull the burlap taut.

Secure the outer hoop by tightening the screw. Create a bow with the burlap ribbon following the instructions on pages 12–15. Use hot glue to attach the bow to the top of the hoop, covering the screw.

**5**

# Pleated ribbon
## TREE SKIRT

### MATERIALS LIST

2 yards (1.8m) gray burlap

10 yards (9m) white burlap ribbon 2"–3" (5cm–8cm) wide

gray thread for sewing machine

white thread for sewing machine

marker or pencil

string

sharp fabric scissors

tape measure

straight pins

sewing machine

When decorating for the holidays, you always have your favorite items you look forward to seeing each year. Soon this tree skirt will be your new favorite piece. You can make it even more special by stenciling a holiday greeting or your family name on the burlap.

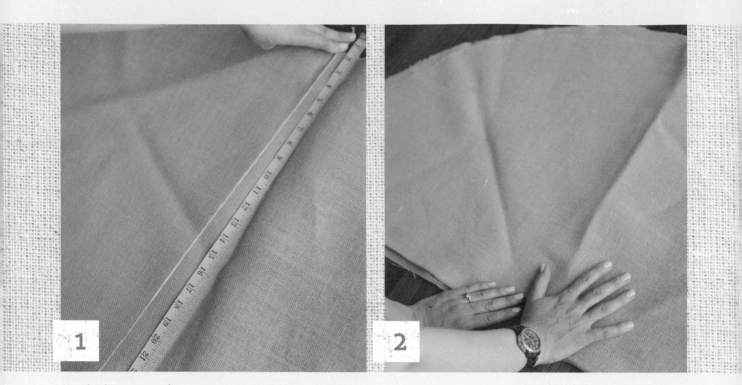

**1** Attach a long piece of string around a marker or pencil. From the marker, measure 24" (61cm) and cut the string. Pin the end of the string to the center of your burlap fabric. Pull the string tight and move the marker in a circle to mark the perimeter of the tree skirt on the burlap.

**2** Use scissors to cut around the perimeter line, making a perfect circle.

Fold the circle of fabric in half three times.

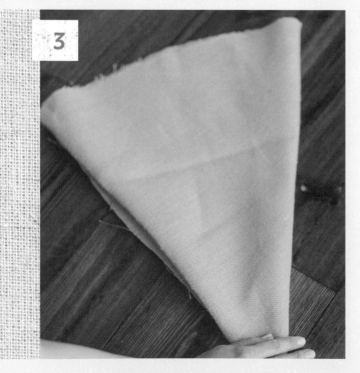

**3**

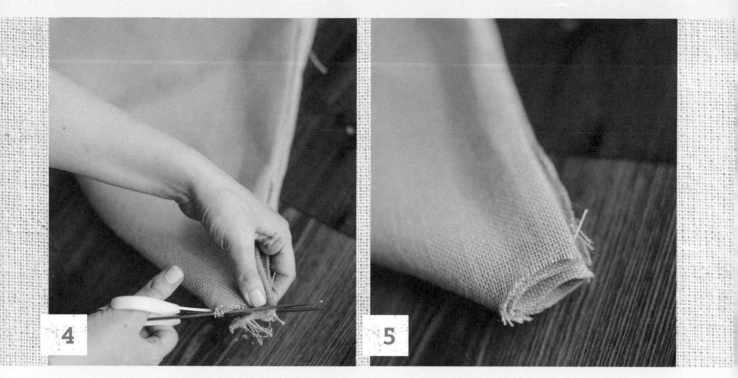

<table>
<tr><td>**4**</td><td>**5**</td></tr>
</table>

Using sharp fabric scissors, cut the tip of the fabric in a curved line (or *U* shape) to make the inner hole for the tree skirt.

The tree trunk will fit through the hole.

Open the fabric and cut a straight line from the outside of the skirt to the center hole. Follow the threads of the burlap to make the line straight.

**6**

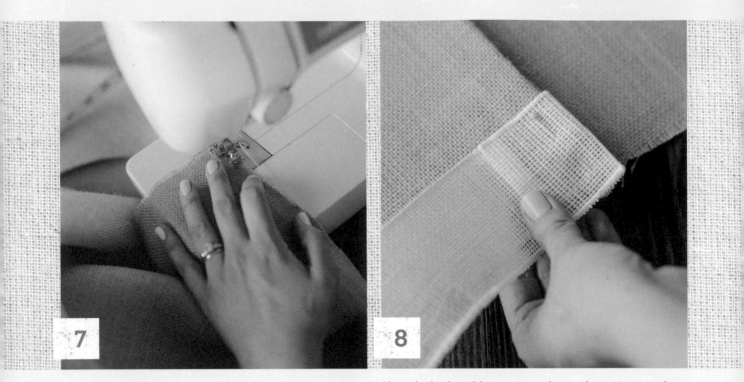

Using your sewing machine and gray thread, sew a zigzag stitch around the perimeter of the skirt, around the interior circle of the skirt, and on both sides of the cut you made in step 6.

Place the burlap ribbon so it overhangs the perimeter edge of the skirt to hide the raw edge. Align the short end of the ribbon with the cut straight line. Pin the ribbon end in place.

Measure 2" (5cm) from the ribbon end, and at that spot, fold the ribbon onto itself by ½" (1cm) to create a pleat. Pin the fold in place.

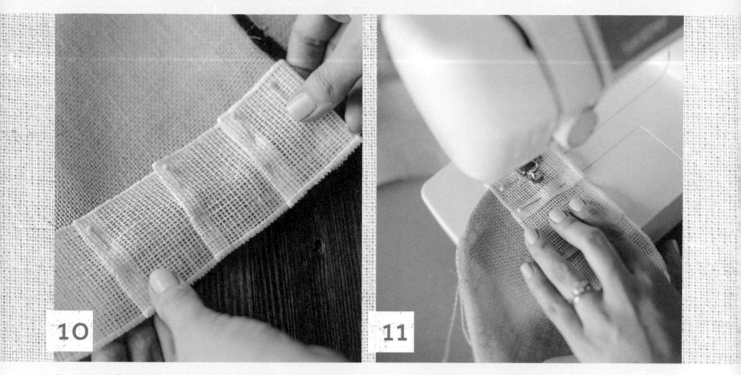

**10** Continue to fold and pin, creating a pleat every 2" (5cm) all around the perimeter of the tree skirt. Repeat around the inside circle.

**11** With white thread, sew a straight stitch down the center (horizontally) of the pleated ribbon to secure it. Remove the pins. Repeat for the inner circle ribbon.

Personalize your tree skirt by stenciling your family name or a holiday greeting on the burlap. See page 11 for instructions for stenciling.

# Christmas
## STOCKING

## MATERIALS LIST

burlap flower

½ yard (.5m) natural burlap

1 yard (0.9m) white burlap ribbon

6" (15cm) jute rope twine

tan and white thread for sewing machine

scissors

tape measure

sewing machine

straight pins

hot glue gun and glue sticks

marker

stocking pattern on page 107

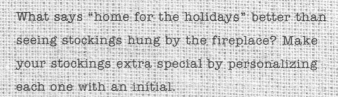

What says "home for the holidays" better than seeing stockings hung by the fireplace? Make your stockings extra special by personalizing each one with an initial.

1

2

Enlarge the stocking pattern on page 107 and trace it onto pattern paper. Cut out the stocking pattern. Place the pattern onto the burlap and trace around it with a marker.

Repeat to trace a second stocking shape. If you're using a printed burlap fabric, flip the pattern over before tracing the second stocking shape.

Cut out both of the outlined stockings.

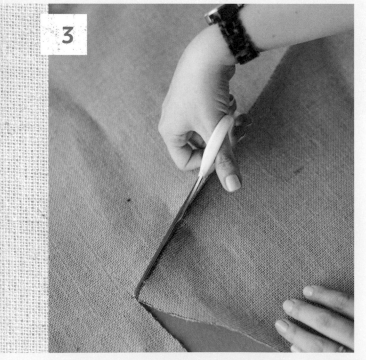

3

**4**

Measure ½" (1cm) from the top edge of both stocking pieces and fold over the edge.

**5**

Pin both folds in place.

Sew down the folds using a straight stitch on your sewing machine and tan thread.

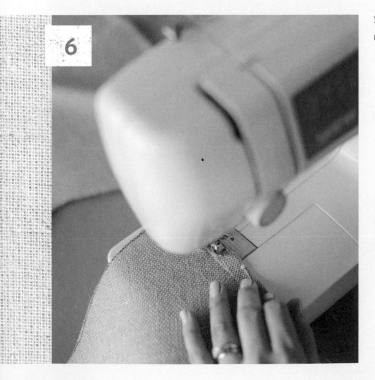

**6**

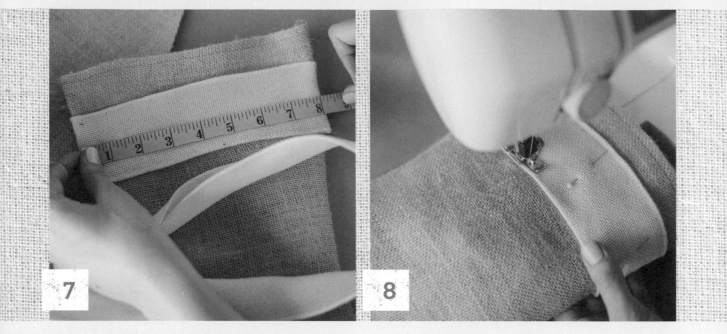

**7** Place a strip of white burlap ribbon 2" (5cm) from the top edge of each stocking. Cut the ribbon to the width of the stocking and pin it in place. Make sure the ribbon is placed on the side of each stocking piece that will face out when the stocking is sewn together.

**8** Sew along both long edges of the ribbon to secure it in place with white thread.

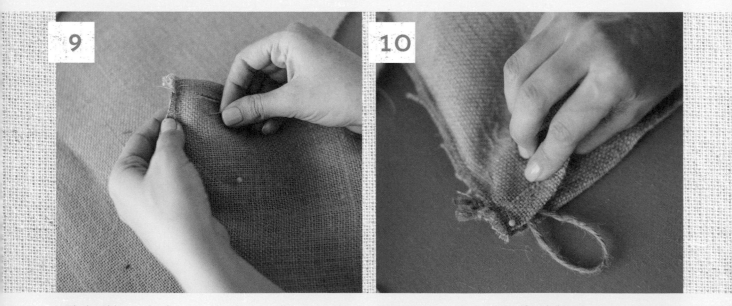

**9** With the ribbon sides facing each other, pin the two stocking pieces together, matching the shapes.

**10** Fold the piece of twine in half and slide the loop inside the stocking at the top corner, opposite the toe. Allow the raw loop ends to hang slightly outside the stocking seam line where the stocking will be sewn, then pin it in place. (When you turn the stocking right-side out, this will become the inside.)

**11**

Using a zigzag stitch on your sewing machine and tan thread, sew from one top corner of the stocking, around the toe, up to the other top corner. Create a ½" (1cm) seam allowance.

**12**

Turn the stocking right-side out. Place hot glue on the back of the burlap flower.

Glue the flower on one side of the stocking in the same corner as the hanging loop.

**13**

## TRIANGLE PATTERN

Triangle pattern for the *Giving Thanks Banner* on page 84.
Shown at 100%.

Burlap boutique

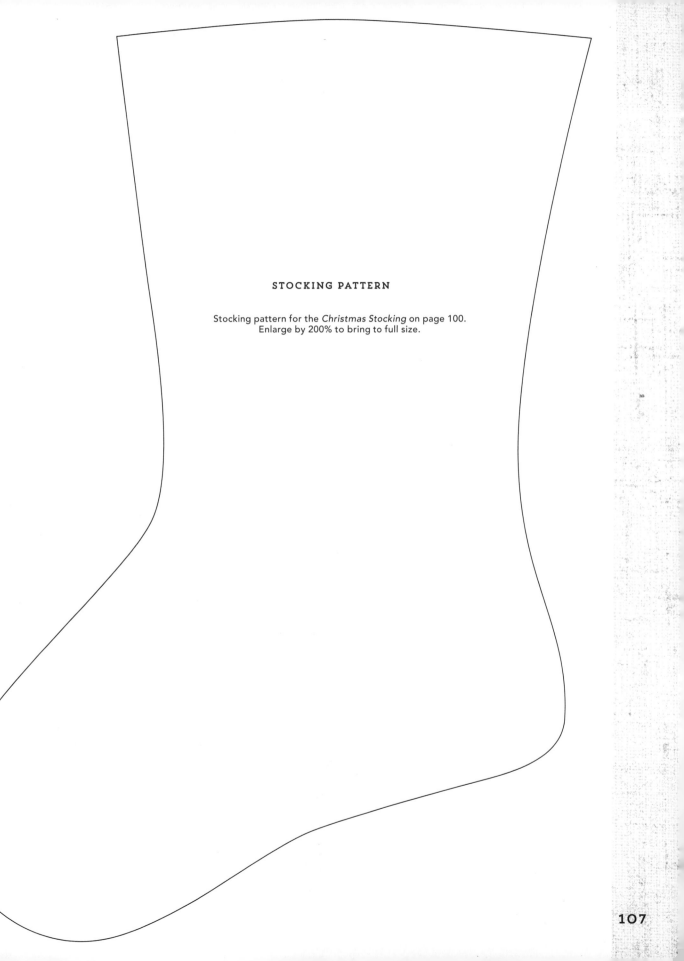

## STOCKING PATTERN

Stocking pattern for the *Christmas Stocking* on page 100.
Enlarge by 200% to bring to full size.

# RESOURCES

The products used in this book are available from your local craft and hobby store, fabric shop or favorite online retailer. To learn more about the products used, visit the websites of the manufacturers listed below.

**ANNIE SLOAN**

www.anniesloan.com

**BROTHER**

www.brother-usa.com

**FISKARS**

www.fiskars.com

**JAMES THOMPSON**

www.jamesthompson.com

# INDEX

Other fine Fons & Porter books are available from your favorite bookstore, fabric or craft store or online supplier.

 www.fwcommunity.com

19  18  17  16  15  5  4  3  2  1

ISBN: 978-1-4402-4151-2
SRN: T2391

Distributed in Canada by Fraser Direct
100 Armstrong Avenue
Georgetown, ON, Canada  L7G 5S4
Tel:  (905) 877-4411

Distributed in the U.K. and Europe
by F&W Media International
LTD Brunel House, Forde Close, Newton Abbot,
TQ12 4PU, UK
Tel: (+44) 1626 323200, Fax: (+44) 1626 323319
Email: enquiries@fwmedia.com

Distributed in Australia by Capricorn Link
P.O. Box 704, S. Windsor NSW, 2756 Australia
Tel: (02) 4560-1600    Fax: (02) 4577-5288
Email: books@capricornlink.com.au

## METRIC CONVERSION CHART

| TO CONVERT | TO | MULTIPLY BY |
| --- | --- | --- |
| Inches | Centimeters | 2.54 |
| Centimeters | Inches | 0.4 |
| Feet | Centimeters | 30.5 |
| Centimeters | Feet | 0.03 |
| Yards | Meters | 0.9 |
| Meters | Yards | 1.1 |

**EDITED BY** Noel Rivera and Christine Doyle
**INTERIOR DESIGN BY** Karla Baker
**COVER DESIGN BY** Kelly Pace
**PHOTOGRAPHY BY** Jeremy Harwell
**PRODUCTION COORDINATED BY** Greg Nock

# More great craft titles to try!

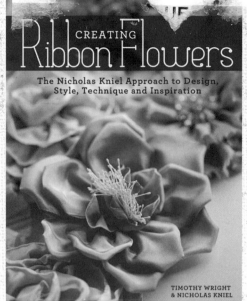

## CRAFT IT NOW

edited by Shannon E. Miller

There you are, enjoying a normal Saturday afternoon, when it hits you: the sudden, inexplicable urge to make something. Whether you're carving a new piece of jewelry or sewing an adorable plush bunny, you'll find something to love in *Craft It Now*. With more than seventy-five simple projects ranging from crochet to polymer clay and everything in between, this book has you covered when you need a quick craft fix.

## CREATING RIBBON FLOWERS

by Timothy Wright and Nicholas Kniel

Nicholas Kniel and Timothy Wright teach their method of creating gorgeous ribbon flowers in this collection of illustrated, step-by-step lessons. With only a few yards of ribbon, you can make the perfect embellishment for any garment, home décor item, wedding party and more.

Find more fun projects at sewdaily.com.

**sew**daily

I dedicate this book to my Grandma Gretchen. She helped instill a love for crafting within me at an early age, and that enthusiasm has continued throughout my entire life.

## ABOUT THE AUTHOR

Katie Carter is a lifelong sewer and crafter. Her Etsy shop, The September Tree, specializes in home décor and wreaths made from burlap. Her work has been featured on dozens of blogs and can be seen in shops and home tours around her home in Georgia. See Katie's latest creations at www.theseptembertree.etsy.com.

## ACKNOWLEDGMENTS

I would like to express my great appreciation to my husband, who has been there to cheer me on and encourage me throughout each day; and to our sons for always being my little helpers and being so patient while inspiring me daily.

I am particularly grateful for the assistance given to me by my mother. She is always there to lend an extra hand on any project or request I give her.

Special thanks to my best friend, Jaclyn Mori, for always pushing me to believe in myself and in all my creative ideas.

To my brother-in-law for his advice, which has been a great help in writing this book.

To the F+W team for seeing my potential and making this book a reality.

To photographer Jeremy Harwell for all the wonderful pictures he worked on so diligently.

To my wonderful editor Christine Doyle for bringing out the best of my words and photographs.

To all of my fans and customers for following my adventures through every post and listing, and for supporting me with each like and sweet comment. Without you all, this book may not have happened.

Last, but certainly not least, I am thankful to the Lord for shaping me into the person I am today. He uses all my imperfections and turns them into good.